Dear Keith

Wishing you great success
In the hybrid!

Debbie

THE
LIVING
ROOM
LEADER

LEADERSHIP LESSONS
FOR A HYBRID FUTURE

THE LIVING ROOM LEADER

LEADERSHIP LESSONS FOR A HYBRID FUTURE

DEBBIE GOODMAN

Requests for permission to make copies of any part of the work
should be emailed to the following address:
Debbie@jhammer.co.za

Published and distributed by Merack Publishing.

Book Design by Kory Kirby
SET IN MINION PRO

Library of Congress Control Number: 2021912100

Goodman, Debbie

THE LIVING ROOM LEADER:
Leadership Lessons for a Hybrid Future

ISBN 978-1-949635-55-3 (Paperback)
ISBN 978-1-949635-57-7 (Hardcover)
ISBN 978-1-949635-56-0 (eBook)

To my magnificent daughters, Gianna and Malia.
You continue to inspire me, every single day.

And thank you, my darlings, for being the best zoom-schoolers a mom could wish to have during a global pandemic! You made my job of trying to be a good living room leader SO much easier.

CONTENTS

INTRODUCTION

AFTER SETTLING INTO THE NEW YEAR OF 2020, MARCH STRUCK with a vengeance. An unprecedented vengeance, altering our lives in a way not experienced in recent history.

The COVID pandemic and resulting measures taken to "flatten the curve"—a term that became part of everyday lexicon within hours—saw many of us become Living Room Leaders overnight. Depending on circumstances, some of us became Bedroom, Garage, Kitchen or even Huddled-inside-a-car-to-get-some-silence Leaders. We had to figure out new ways to manage people and logistics, and after that, ways to manage, motivate, hire and engage our teams. All this with no road map, no "best practice" guidelines, no historic precedent and no "how to lead remote teams RIGHT NOW" training manual.

Some of us may have been working diligently towards lofty goals such as flexi-time and work-from-home options for our teams as motivational and retention strategies. We were looking towards a leadership style and approach that would cultivate greater accountability from everyone—and in turn greater trust, communication, collaboration and of course greater productivity. But none of us expected to have to achieve this over a weekend!

Personally, I had already been working remotely for more than a couple of years, due to a move across the Atlantic from my office in Cape Town, to my new home office in Los Angeles. Prior to the relocation, I had spent the better part of six months figuring out how to transition from being in the office full-time, to full-time remote working (including a significant time zone difference). This required a fairly substantial change process for myself and my team. Overall, I'd say my team accomplished this pretty well, but it had taken six months, lots of planning, and additional support from business coaches and best practice leadership frameworks and tools. Not the ridiculously short notice that we were all given to batten down the hatches at home!

In fact, had you asked any corporate executive or entrepreneur managing teams in February 2020 how long they thought it might take to have everyone ready to work from home in a sustainable and productive way, answers would likely have ranged from, "Not possible for everyone to work from home regardless of the circumstances," to "Three to six months minimum."

Yet, there we were. Faced with lockdown or shelter-in-place orders all over the world, requiring almost everyone in professional, non-essential worker roles or industries to WORK FROM HOME WITH IMMEDIATE EFFECT—regardless of the level of preparedness.

The Living Room Leader is my account of the shifts and changes that I and many of my peers—leaders in corporations and entrepreneurs running a range of differently sized organizations—had to make in record time in order to survive. Some barely managed, but others managed to thrive during what was, and remains, undoubtedly the most challenging work-life experience that any of us have ever encountered.

This is a story about leadership. About how ordinary people like you and I found ourselves thrust into our living rooms, bedrooms, garages, or walk-in-closets. (Yes, I've encountered a few who found themselves in said room so as not to have their home-schooling kids Zoom-bomb their meetings.) About how we had to figure out how to manage our teams remotely, how to hire new people without ever having met them in person, and how to engage them and help them remain productive. But the story is not just retrospective. It's one that is evolving as I write, while we're experiencing "third waves" and new virus variants in many places in the world, concurrent with vaccine rollouts that are being administered with increasing efficacy in some countries, and severe challenges in others.

On one hand, the impact of potentially yet another phase of lockdown sometime in the future is adding renewed mental and emotional stress and fatigue to people who are already stretched very thin in this domain. On the other hand, the availability of the vaccine is driving confidence that life will be returning to some kind of semi-normality in the foreseeable future.

What life and work will look like next month, or the month after that, is still anyone's guess—particularly if you are not yet in the privileged position of being in line for a shot in the arm. I have never before felt such intense time pressure to write and publish content, being acutely aware that this book might be entirely out of date and irrelevant if I don't move fast enough, due to the rapid changes occurring in the world, and the world of work, right now. Yet, while writing under this pressure, it's also becoming clear that some of the lessons we have learned are lessons that will no doubt persist in years to come, even if COVID is miraculously vanquished in its entirety tomorrow.

So while a retrospective look at this last year in the workplace derivative is certainly noteworthy, my focus for *The Living Room Leader* is on the lessons learned, and the new paths forged during this extraordinary time, that might—and in my view, should—sustain beyond this era of the pandemic.

The backstory to *The Living Room Leader* is that I had a different book (one which I'd spent most of 2019 writing) waiting with the publishers—literally days before lockdown/shelter-in-place became our reality. I had a sense of foreboding that things were about to change fundamentally in the world, and that the book that I'd spent so many hours writing was likely to become (at least partially) redundant overnight. I told the publishers to press the pause button. Just over a year later, the pause button has now been substituted for the halt-indefinitely button.

By the time I caught my breath last year after disaster struck—after the cost cutting exercises had been done, the risk mitigation strategies had been implemented, and the attempts at forecasting and scenario planning had been conducted (oh, what a laugh in retrospect, scenario planning for a global pandemic!)—life and work as we knew it had indeed already gone through so much change. Some of which we now know will be long lasting and redefine the future of work. So, with much of the earlier book binned—and only the material that I believe will likely continue to have relevance during and after COVID retained—I set out to gather new material.

One of the perks of being in the business of leadership is that I have access to some pretty extraordinary and innovative leaders all over the world. From the early days of work-from-home, I began to interview them to hear how they had responded to the crisis, and how they had leveraged the COVID landscape to achieve some unexpected positive outcomes with their teams.

My interest (and inspiration) lies in some of the new practices and ways of leading, hiring and engaging that leaders have implemented during the crisis that they continue to develop and evolve. My view is that even when we're through this, some of "the new" will hopefully become "the norm" into the future.

Strategies that might have worked a year ago pre-COVID, now need a complete rethink. Even that which seemed to suffice in the early days of COVID might no longer be doing the trick.

Regardless of whether we're still in this for three, six, or nine months longer (or more), it's not too late to start implementing some of the impactful changes that other companies started a while back.

And it's certainly not too late to ask provocative questions like these, inspired by Seth Godin:

"If we're not buying or selling hours, what, exactly do we measure and how are we compensated for it?... **And if we are**

buying and selling hours, how does that work when sur-
veillance capitalism bumps into workers needing flexible
schedules and the trust that it takes to develop leadership
and creative contribution?"

Adding to this, I have some questions of my own: What
might arise if we are able to co-create, with our colleagues,
work-lives where we are all functioning in our zones of excellence—doing jobs that we're well-suited to, working with peers
and leaders who we trust, and for a mission or vision that
matters to us—what then is possible?'

Whilst these notions may sound like lofty ideals, I see leaders
of the 'love and loyalty' variety all around. They may not be in
the spotlight, on a speakers' platform, or hailed as leadership
gurus, but they're nonetheless inspiring for the way in which
they have helped their teams thrive, just by applying what I
consider to be 'the basics'. I'll share some of this too, later in
the book. While there's less novelty here, these may be of even
greater impact to you—because if you're not already incorpo-
rating some of these team rituals and practices, now's as good
a time as any to start. And there's definitely some peace of
mind to be found in realising the continued value of familiar
practices that have stood the test of time.

"The fundamental job of a leader is to...help people grow to their fullest human potential"

—FRED REICHHELD

*New York Times best-selling author,
creator Net Promoter system*

My assumption is that if you're reading this book, you're either a "lifelong learner" (always interested in increasing your knowledge and skill as a leader, as really all leaders should be) or you're having some challenges with leading your team, combined with uncertainty about the future. Either way, I'm hopeful that *The Living Room Leader* will help you to develop your leadership skills, make really great hiring decisions in the context of hybrid—or even fully remote—work, and ensure that your teams are engaged, productive and happy.

One thing is certain: this global pandemic is going to leave an indelible mark on all of our lives, and in particular our working lives. Whether widely available access to a vaccine means the end is in sight remains to be seen. In the meantime, let's buckle up and excel at leading from whichever room in the house we happen to find ourselves.

CHAPTER 1

DON'T SQUANDER THE MOMENT

NONE OF US ASKED FOR THIS, BUT WE ALL HAD TO PLAY THE hand we were dealt. With the initial phase of survival behind us, we can now look forward to how we can start rebuilding given our recent historical context—and without falling back into the practices that did not serve us in the past. One of the key messages that emerged from my discussions with leaders since the early days of COVID is the need to determine how you continue into the future, not only ensuring that business remains sustainable, but also searching for opportunities that may have arisen. Put bluntly—you are in a position to achieve the extraordinary. And if not the extraordinary, at least something fresh that leaves you and your team better positioned to manage the challenges that are yet to come, and to exploit opportunities that may arise.

As I re-read leadership articles from the earlier days of COVID, such as McKinsey's quarterly report *The CEO Moment: Leadership for a new era*[1] (July 2020), I found myself inspired once more by the stories of CEOs who managed to leverage opportunities presented by COVID to achieve extraordinary

1 Dewar, Carolyn, Scott Keller, Kevin Sneader, and Kurt Strovink. "The CEO Moment: Leadership for a New Era." McKinsey & Company. McKinsey & Company, February 11, 2021. https://www.mckinsey.com/featured-insights/leadership/the-ceo-moment-leadership-for-a-new-era.

shifts, changes, goals, and milestones—opportunities they never even realised existed pre-pandemic.

Indeed, COVID is being hailed as an accelerant towards glory or demise. Some companies have performed beyond their wildest dreams, while others have unfortunately not shared in this fortune, instead imploding in a poof of smoke. The glorious ones are noted in the McKinsey report, so no need for repetition here (but definitely worth the read if you've not done so already).

What's probably more commonplace though, are the countless companies that have achieved neither greatness nor obsolescence during this time, yet managed to survive, counting themselves lucky to still be around. These companies and their leadership teams have done nothing startlingly good or bad, but they managed to keep the wheels turning, and their heads are still above water—that in itself is worthy of a pat on the back given the circumstances. If your company is still around at this stage of the game, I'm willing to applaud and throw roses. Well done!

Yet there may still be an opportunity for you, your people and your company to achieve something superb. While the urgency of the early days may have passed (many of the incredible shifts made by the CEOs noted in the McKinsey report and others were due to the time-sensitivity and radical change of EVERYTHING almost overnight), there is still time to dig deep and assess what new opportunities have arisen that you can capitalize on right now.

"In any moment of decision, the best thing you can do is the right thing, the next best thing is the wrong thing, and the worst thing you can do is nothing."

—THEODORE ROOSEVELT

Instead of thinking about how you can "get back to normal," challenge yourself *and* your people to keep stretching towards a new paradigm.

Because while you may have made it to this point—and feel like if you got this far you're in the clear—the fact is that the world has changed irrevocably, and so it's still imperative that you stress-test your business and people fundamentals in the context of some key variables in order to assess and ensure future viability.

These variables include:

CONSUMER BEHAVIOUR

Consumer behaviour has undergone a major change, most notably with regards to online shopping. Ecommerce has truly come into its own during COVID, and any direct-to-consumer business will need to take into account this change—which is unlikely to be reversed—into the future. Just because we *can* go to the mall doesn't mean we will. Yes, this type of entertainment experience may be sustained for the purposes of gathering and communing with friends, but many have discovered the convenience, ease and relative affordability of being able to shop online.

ARTIFICIAL INTELLIGENCE AND AUTOMATION

As noted in the World Economic Forum's most recent Future of Jobs report[2] (2020), AI and automation are going to continue

---

2 "The Future of Jobs Report 2020." World Economic Forum. Accessed June 10, 2021. https://www.weforum.org/reports/the-future-of-jobs-report-2020.

driving all areas of business and life. While there may have been a momentary glance away from the impact of AI last year while our attention was focused elsewhere, do not be deluded into thinking that perhaps it was a fad. AI is here to stay and grow.

NEW NORMS OF TRAVEL AND WORK

This includes traveling FOR work. Business travel is likely to continue to be hugely impacted in the short term, but many sources are saying that traveling for meetings and conferences in the same way as we did pre-COVID is not likely to return—regardless of increasing safety measures and vaccinations. Traveling to the office (when this presents a sizable chunk of your day) will also no longer happen on a regular basis. We're already seeing how this has impacted nomadic and online workstyles, the need for proximity between home and office, and the preference for homes that offer additional space.

Just because you're still here is no assurance that you're here to stay. We've been speaking of disruption and exponential growth of technology for several years—decades, in fact. COVID partly reduced airtime on the topic of disruption, but in many respects has been the ultimate disrupter.

So now is the time to dig deep AGAIN, and check the horizon for changes, threats and opportunities.

One of the biggest opportunities lies in the next phase of what may indeed become a sustainable way of working—namely, "the hybrid"—and will require a personalized, flexible, adaptable approach to leadership.

As Living Room Leaders—who will shortly be heading into some kind of semi, demi, half, hybrid work scenario—what are the lessons we have learned that we will take with us into the hybrid era, to make all of our work-lives healthier, happier and more fulfilling?

Rethinking and planning for the future may feel like an exhausting exercise at this moment in time, as the iterations and revisions seem endlessly changing with new variables (and 'variants') being thrown into the mix, tossing even the best laid plans up in the air.

Yet there are some certainties that we can bank on: people want to feel fulfilled by the work that they do. They want to work with leaders and peers who they trust. They want to know that they are valued and that their work matters.

Increasingly, people at all levels of an organisation want and expect both agency and meaning in their work. In the hybrid, professional and personal aspects of life will continue to meld and merge, more so than ever before, and so we owe it to ourselves—and ultimately to all of our stakeholders—to think deeply about the possibilities that a hybrid future offers to cultivate amazing, enriching workplaces, where everyone thrives.

CHAPTER 2

LOCKDOWN: THE ULTIMATE OFF-SITE TEAM BUILDER

THE EARLY DAYS OF THE COVID LOCKDOWNS WERE CHARACTERIZED
by an unprecedented global fight-or-flight response. There was
an adrenaline rush as our survival instinct kicked in, forcing
organizations to put in place those measures that might have
long been on the discussion table. Without a doubt, our new landscape offered us the opportunity for a clean slate. The chance to start thinking and doing differently, albeit under duress.

Just like an off-site strategy session, right?

Think about it, lockdown as a gigantic, global off-site team-building session! Granted, no fancy resort (unfortunately) or plush conference facilities (quite the opposite, as we know.) But with the same impact that a shift in physical space and working conditions is known to have—creativity and innovation.

All of us, simultaneously and concurrently, were faced with a change in environment and the way we do things, and as a result, there was a heightening of energy and an extreme focus on getting things done. The good leaders among us applied laser-like attention to their people and their efforts to figure out the challenge, which sparked new (and often more effective) strategies for continuing operations.

Despite the fear and uncertainty, or perhaps because of it, employee productivity spiked in some organizations, as people sought to protect their livelihoods against the odds. There was an extreme willingness to put their bodies on the line—many literally, but for most of us figuratively—and to go above and beyond the normal call of duty. It was an all-hands-on-deck situation.

The fear of losing their jobs meant that most employees were willing and open to work longer and harder, and to do whatever it took to ensure the continued viability of the organization.

Where in the past, managers were hesitant to consider remote working due to the fear of a drop in productivity, they now had to devise ways to ensure continued engagement by putting in place effective communication strategies, and providing constant feedback.

MOST OF ALL, TRUST BECAME PARAMOUNT

The "bums-on-seats" mentality was given a swift kick in the pants. Leaders who had previously feared the possibility of treating their teams as grownups working towards a common goal, were now forced to deal with their concerns with little in the way of mental preparation.

Anecdotal evidence suggests that this culture shift has, in many cases, been successful, resulting in greater team cohesion and trust among co-workers and management.

And how did this happen? Through a daily process of seeing

one another, as human beings, by stepping into each other's lives through our screens in a way that would have been impossible in the office-only environment.

We saw each other's homes, families, pets, babies and shared in each other's struggles that normally would have been left at home. For a year or so, the home and work switch did not exist.

Many organizations proclaim to have cultures that value compassion and empathy, integrity and trust. But the working conditions imposed by COVID were truly a stress test of culture. Indeed, only in a crisis do we have the opportunity to put our words and proclamations to the test. Companies and teams who had a truly tight-knit culture before, emerged as the easy winners, with teams working together successfully.

In these "golden teams," managers trusted people to get on with things, people were empowered to ask for help, take time off, work at odd hours (or whatever else was needed to be productive), and everyone stepped up with solutions-based thinking. There was the added element of a "looking out" for each other mindset—both personally and professionally.

For some organizations, as I saw in my own, the culture deepened even further because of the added human connection. There was a shared threat to be dealt with, and office politics were served a body blow.

The playing field was by no means even, but one of the benefits of the experience was that teams could see their managers deal with many of the same issues they were facing themselves, and managers had to make major efforts to ensure that their employees were doing okay. As a result of this shared struggle, we cultivated more compassion, new seeds were sown, and we had an increasing awareness of our shared humanity.

BANKING THE GAINS

These gains run the risk of becoming a historical event (with some sentimentality attached to lockdown memories) if we emerge into a post-COVID world and close the door behind us without reviewing the lessons and banking the gains. That wouldn't make much sense, given what we know now. So, what do we retain and take into the future?

For each of us, there will be something different, based on our vision for the future. But now that we know what is possible, it's the responsibility of each of us to take stock and move forward, preserving the best of what this gruelling time has offered.

For weeks, I had been dreading having 'the conversation' with my colleagues. With our business revenues and volumes having fallen off a cliff within a short period after lockdown, I'd spent hours and hours working with our CFO on cash flow models and projections, looking at all the possible costs to cut, and determining line items that were essential versus nice-to-have luxuries in the context of severely reduced earnings.

At the end of this exercise, I was faced with an excruciating decision—retrench one or two people, or ask everyone in the company to take a pay-cut. The idea of retrenching or furloughing even one team mate was so awful to me, that I chickened out on taking this decision alone, and instead scheduled one-to-one calls with everyone in the company.

"We have a tough decision to make, retrench someone or take a pay-cut. What should we do?" was the question I put to each one. And, true to form, every single person in the company elected to take a salary sacrifice rather than see one of their work-friends out of a job.

It was a proud and humbling moment for me, to see the depth of care and compassion that my work-family had (and continue to have) for one another, and the strength of trust that they displayed in me to lead them through some very uncertain and bleak months.

CHAPTER 3

THE PRODUCTIVITY PARADOX AND THE VALUE OF THE POST-PANDEMIC OFFICE

THE FIRST CHANGE TO PRESERVE IS A RETHINK OF THE post-pandemic office in creative, new ways. And central to this is the consideration of the value of the physical office and its impact on performance and productivity.

Issues many executive teams and chief risk officers had previously spent countless hours grappling with—what if a disaster should strike and we need to hunker down somewhere outside of our offices?—turned out to be relatively simple to sort out logistically, all things considered. Send the people home, give them laptops and data, and if they need to be there for a while, make sure that they have an ergonomic chair to sit on in front of their dressing table in their bedrooms.

All in all, vacating offices and shifting to work-from-home was done with relative degrees of precision, and most companies found a groove while ensuring the productivity of their teams within weeks of the exodus.

Very quickly, remote work due to COVID exposed the inadequacies of compulsory office attendance. The days of defaulting to an office, of commuting for hours daily (with no one ever challenging this practice), are things of the past. Which is not to say that there isn't a case to be made for physical presence in the office. But face time during office hours can no longer be considered a valid metric relating to performance—even for the most die-hard command-and-control manager.

WHEN THE CAT'S AWAY...

A commonly held assumption among many managers I've interviewed over the years is that when the metaphorical cat is away, the mice will play. Loosely translated—if people are not being actively monitored or overseen in the physical presence of the boss, they'll likely slack off. Performance will lag and productivity will plummet if they feel that no one is watching.

As it turns out, for the most part, such disasters did not transpire. In fact, through my anecdotal interviews for this book—and the many studies that have been conducted along the way—I learned the productivity scale, or range of performance and output, remained intact. Those who previously were highly motivated and engaged continued to achieve and succeed (some even more so) within this new environment.

Similarly, the lower end performers continued to have low productivity. Of course, both groups and the ones hanging about in the middle of this continuum were impacted by external circumstances—including issues around schooling, home environment, tech challenges, space, health matters and so forth. However, even taking these challenges into account, the general trend as it existed in the office, remained to be mostly true for the range of performers as they worked from home.

(Even though there was heightened productivity among most people at the start of lockdown, for reasons discussed elsewhere.)

So if what we're now seeing is that environment does not have as significant an impact on performance and productivity as we may previously have believed, two main questions arise:

1. What are the variables we should be focusing on now to support and enhance productivity?
2. What is the actual value of the physical office in the new era of work?

ENHANCING PRODUCTIVITY — WHAT DO WE DO NOW?

In my introductory chapter, I mentioned that some of what we should do going forward is more about going back to basics than plucking some new innovation out of the COVID ether. And never more so than with this point around productivity. In a nutshell, it's all about the people, and having the right people for your company doing the right jobs. Not every exceptionally talented person is going to automatically succeed in your organization. Nor will every person who might be a great fit for your company automatically succeed in their role if they're not doing the job that's right for them at that point in their career.

So, the back to basics answer is—make sure that you're hiring the right people! Because when you get FIT right (job-fit and culture-fit) performance will skyrocket, regardless of environment.

Of course, getting fit right can be a fine balancing act, which requires some mastery and finesse—a matter I discuss later in this book, in Chapter 10. But it's clear that the basic answer to the complex productivity question lies in making great hiring decisions.

TO OFFICE OR NOT TO OFFICE — THAT IS THE QUESTION

With productivity no longer the rationale behind gathering at the office every weekday for a minimum of eight hours a day, it is worth reflecting on the value that offices DO hold. In the past, office attendance was the default setting—because that was the way we worked and it was written into our contracts. The office was where we went to get our jobs done. Now that an unprecedented number of employees (not just the select few working under special dispensation) have experienced the benefits of remote working, it is clear that the prevailing nine-to-five office culture died in March 2020.

In the post-pandemic future of work, nine out of ten organizations will be combining remote and on-site working[3].

3 "What Executives Are Saying about the Future of Hybrid Work." McKinsey & Company. McKinsey & Company, June 8, 2021. https://www.mckinsey.com/business-functions/organization/our-insights/what-executives-are-saying-about-the-future-of-hybrid-work?cid=other-eml-nsl-mip-mck&hlkid=22f64a2f129542a5950a0dc7f58c2385&hctky=11601495&hdpid=ceff44f0-dfbd-435e-ac8c-852e9afcf44f.

So in making decisions about the future of your company's home/office work strategy, there are a range of variables that should be considered, including: team morale and culture, onboarding and training of new staff members, project collaboration and idea generation, as well as the learning and growth we all experience by being in the presence of talented, creative co-workers.

The office is essentially a learning hub. Sharing organizational knowledge and passing it on to the next generation of leaders cannot be done purely through remote work, as learning often happens by osmosis, through ad hoc office meetings and collaborations, and by overhearing comments and telephone conversations.

Experts agree that the office will therefore become a purposeful space, that we'll go there out of necessity for something specific rather than by default. It will need to be reconfigured ergonomically and will need to include more inviting social spaces. This will feed into attracting future talent too, as employees will ask themselves, "what's in it for me?" as they question why they need to commute to a space when then they could easily work from home.

MAKING THE CALL

Making a call on the best balance of these variables can be primarily determined by asking the following questions:

- What value does physically being in the office bring to our people, and our organization?
- Have we been able to replicate this in a remote work setup? What strategies have been most effective, and could we maximize these?
- If we were to remain primarily as remote workers, what would the impact be? Can we quantify both the negative and positive impact of this?
- If we return in part (or in some hybrid form), what would we REALLY want to use our in-office time for?

THE ROLE OF LEADERS

Success in a remote, distributed workforce can be achieved—both at an individual and organizational level—but it requires strong leadership. Our COVID work experiences showed us that performance *can* be monitored by output and not by presence alone, so the simple answer to the productivity question is actually twofold, the right people and strong leadership.

SO WHAT'S NEXT?

"Some bosses are demanding workers return to the office, and some managers have spent the last year forcing people to endure endless zoom meetings.

But as it gets easier to measure productivity and contribution, and as it gets easier to outsource any task that can be described clearly, there's a fork in the road."

—SETH GODIN

Organizations and leaders need to seize the moment, as now is the time to intentionally consider how they want to evolve into the future. This is a significant shift for the workforce and, like so much else at this time, its success rests on decisive leadership. By doing the hard work upfront—such as formally defining new ways of working, setting expectations for what good flexibility looks like, investing in the technology needed to make employees effective in a virtual world and, of course, leading the way by visibly role-modelling what this looks like—it will equip organizations and teams for success.

PRACTICAL MATTERS

Some of the iterations we've already seen for back-to-work across the globe include the following:

- **Shared workspaces:** For multi-site companies with offices in many locations, some are offering a "hot desk" or shared workspace setup that allows staff to work at the office closest to their home. Alternatively, staff can work from a shared workspace (not owned by the company) close to home, to help those who have unsuitable WFH setups.
- **Fruit salad:** Staff can decide which days they'd like to be in office, randomly and according to what works best for them and the company.
- **Set days in and out:** Teams decide when the whole team will be in the office for "collaboration days." These

include days for strategy sessions and other group work that teams find easier to do in person.

- **Four in, one home:** Some companies are expecting their people to be in the office four out of five days a week, as a concession to those who have enjoyed the WFH flexibility.

- **All in, eventually:** There are some companies who have been crystal clear that they eventually expect everyone to go back to the office full-time, as and when it is safe to do so. Already, many companies have called on all employees to return to the office. While others are not pressuring people to go back just yet, they have managed their teams' expectations around the future—as in, NO work from home at all. At least this provides some certainty for those who were considering moving to a less urban (and less expensive) area.

- **Full WFH:** And then there are those who have fully embraced WFH, and are getting rid of their office space entirely!

The key is to ask the right questions for YOUR company and team before deciding on what the future will look like for your workplace. Most importantly, do not simply default to the way things were a year ago, or decide on a policy without consultation.

CHAPTER 4

HOW COVID BECAME THE CATALYST FOR NEW WAYS OF WORKING

ASIDE FROM THE OBVIOUS MASSIVE CHANGE TO WORKING remotely, and the shifts in work rhythm and style that this brought about, several leaders saw unanticipated innovations that are definitely worth considering as we emerge into hybrid work models.

PERFECT IS THE ENEMY OF DONE

Never before has this maxim become clearer than during COVID. Over the years, in many organizations I've seen a reluctance on the part of employees to share unfinished or imperfect work—mostly because submitting work that is unpolished would be heavily sanctioned (overtly or covertly, or maybe just in the mind of the procrastinator). People were loath to show and tell prematurely for fear of negative judgment and the repercussions that would come from work that might be considered sub-par.

This subliminal fear of imperfection or error often co-exists in the very same companies who profess to follow an ethos of making mistakes as part of a learning culture, and of beta testing new ideas in order to innovate.

Compound this with feedback sessions that are usually not occurring in a cadence that keeps work flowing and moving at a good pace. What typically happens as a result, is that progress is slower and more ponderous than it should be. It takes longer to submit work because the need for perfection and final drafting means a much greater investment of time. It also takes longer to receive feedback and iterate because feedback loops are delayed.

FREQUENT, FAST FEEDBACK

Everyone I interviewed consistently spoke about implementing a new, more frequent meeting rhythm for their teams in the first months of COVID. Leadership teams were meeting daily or weekly instead of monthly, team meetings were taking place with much greater regularity, and even boards were connecting more often—both formally and informally with their peers and colleagues.

The impact of these more frequent—and often shorter— meetings was that people were compelled to show work that was unfinished, still in progress or in rough draft, resulting in quicker feedback and more rapid iterations on ideas in formation.

This was an extremely positive and healthy development, because it allowed iterative, progressive, additive idea generation and ongoing creative collaboration. The focus was on getting things done and making improvements rather than delivering a perfect end product the first time around.

"Done is better than perfect."

—SHERYL SANDBERG

For some companies, this was a completely new way of working and represented a massive culture shift. For others, it was less so, but the speed and urgency with which people were working meant that projects were completed in record time.

Either way, frequent and fast feedback loops are worth keeping in the future, even though the regularity of meetings may have shifted pace from the fight-or-flight urgency of the early days of the pandemic.

DIGITAL DECISION-MAKING

It should go without saying (but I'll say it just in case...) that with people not needing to travel in order to meet and make a decision, and instead achieving the same outcome—a discussion and a decision—pretty much instantly via an online meeting, the speed of decision-making increased.

While there is certainly a case for continued high level, strategic decision-making and thinking, and for discussion and debate to take place face-to-face, when it comes to the hundreds of smaller, transactional decisions that occur in every company daily, I think it would be a shame to revert to old ways of doing things.

Nevertheless, I'm also very aware of the challenges that new teams are experiencing, having recruited and onboarded people remotely over the last year, without ever having met in person. In the absence of innovative onboarding processes that support remote working, or significant time and attention being applied to create connection and cohesive ways of working together, some of these teams are understandably underperforming. Is the remedy for these teams to hustle them back to the office? It may be, but I'd urge some deeper analysis of the underlying issues, before this 'in-office' bandaid is applied.

HARNESS THE GREAT IDEAS THAT COME FROM... EVERYONE!

In addition to speedy decision-making, online meetings also meant much greater access to information and idea generation. Many of my clients in large companies set up regular town halls, discussion groups, or open sessions where staff could ask questions of the CEO, or share ideas.

The initial intention behind some of these large meetings was to address the concerns, fears and anxieties that so many employees were dealing with in the early months of COVID. In many instances, these group calls evolved into something more, and many leaders commented on the benefits of regular engagement with their teams as a way to poll for innovation.

So why stop now? If you found value in these forums, continue with them even as we find a new rhythm with the WFH or back to the office-hybrid. And if you haven't already set up some kind of regular town hall where everyone can connect periodically, do it now!

Surprisingly, what was evident in many of my leadership interviews, is that working in physical isolation resulted in the introduction of vibrant new dynamics in teams—albeit under duress—which saw greater speed and efficiency become the rule rather than the exception. This momentum and back-to-basics approach may yet prove to be the secret ingredient that sees those companies that managed to survive, achieve great new heights as economies open up.

"If you have an apple and I have an apple and we exchange these apples then you and I will still each have one apple. But if you have an idea and I have an idea and we exchange these ideas, then each of us will have two ideas."

—GEORGE BERNARD SHAW

CHAPTER 5

LEADING WITH EMPATHY: THE ULTIMATE GAME CHANGER

OF ALL THE PANDEMIC-RELATED SHIFTS, CHANGES AND innovations I've researched and spoken to leaders about, the most impactful gain cited by almost everyone is the way in which people showed up with empathy and compassion. This leadership quality, empathy—which has been researched and analyzed extensively due to it being considered a core element to a healthy, productive workforce—achieved a pretty big boost during lockdown. Indeed, barriers came crashing down, and personal connection between management and teams became greater than ever before—even though this happened, ironically, while physically separated.

Given the turmoil—personal and professional—faced by all, empathy entered the conversation in a way it had not done before, and there was a much greater willingness to consider the personal circumstances and experiences of employees. Where hyper-personalization arose as a factor in leadership before the pandemic, the experiences of 2020 clearly showed the importance of employee experience in loyalty, productivity and engagement.

"Empathy is about standing in someone else's shoes, feeling with his or her heart, seeing with his or her eyes. Not only is empathy hard to outsource and automate, but it makes the world a better place."

—DANIEL PINK

The work from home situation highlighted the difference between workplaces with leadership philosophies that viewed employees as resources (which just happened to be human) required to deliver output; in juxtaposition with leadership approaches that saw their colleagues as human beings with full lives beyond the workplace.

It seems obvious that the crisis was infinitely more challenging (on every level) for teams lacking connected, empathetic leadership than for those teams and leaders who were already on a path of synergy.

In an effort to shift this conversation from what many might consider to be 'soft stuff' or 'warm and fuzzy' (although I'm assuming if you've read this far, you're of the leadership ilk that knows that the so-called 'soft stuff' is actually what matters most), to some measure of behavioural science, here are insights on leading with empathy, derived from self-determination theory.

AUTONOMY, COMPETENCE AND RELATEDNESS

According to self-determination theory (a macro theory of human motivation and personality related to the inherent psychological needs and striving for growth in humans), there are three psychological needs that are generally universal— autonomy, competence, and relatedness.

Autonomy is the desire to be a causal agent of one's own life and act in harmony with one's integrated self. However, note this does not mean to be independent of others, but rather constitutes a feeling of overall psychological liberty and freedom of internal will. When a person is autonomously motivated, their performance, wellness, and engagement are heightened compared to a person who is told what to do.

Most of us, regardless of the level at which we operate in an organisation, experienced heightened levels of autonomy during the shift to remote work.

Competence is the desire to control the outcome and experience mastery. For instance, it was found that giving people unexpected positive feedback on a task increased people's intrinsic motivation to do it. This was because the positive feedback was fulfilling people's need for competence.

We've spoken about feedback loops and the increased frequency with which this took place, particularly during the early months of work-from-home shifts. So let's tick this box too.

Relatedness is the will to interact with, be connected to, and experience caring for others. In other words – empathy. It shows up in behaviours that demonstrate to others that they matter, that you can relate to their circumstances, and care about their wellbeing.

Without a doubt, relatedness, compassion and empathy amplified and expanded in so many of the workplaces I encountered during my research for this book.

What COVID showed us is that the above human elements amounted to much more than touchy-feely, nice-to-haves unrelated to the bottom line. In fact, it's the teams who were able to stand together in support of each other in a much more open and authentic way, who were able to weather the challenges more successfully.

And yet, of all the gains, expanded empathy is at the greatest risk of being lost or substantially diminished as we head 'back to normal'.

The team check-ins and fun virtual events intended to create a sense of belonging and connectedness have in many instances become a thing of the past. Seldom these days do colleagues hang out for a chat, share a glass of wine or coffee, or participate in a bake-off. These intentional connectors were imperative at the time to deal with isolation, but they also provided opportunities for people at all levels of the organisation to relate to one another.

With the transition into any form of hybrid that doesn't take into account and intentionally provide opportunities for connecting and relating, leaders stand to lose the incredible – albeit unanticipated – gains made in generating compassionate cultures.

My big ask is that 'opportunities for compassionate connecting' will be added to the list of items that require attention for the next phase of hybrid working. What worked well during WFH? And what elements of what worked can be taken into your hybrid future?

CHAPTER 6

MENTAL HEALTH: A DEFINING MOMENT

**FINALLY THERE'S BEEN AN ACKNOWLEDGEMENT THAT MENTAL
and emotional wellbeing is a critical issue to address in the context
of the workplace.**

This of course is nothing new—as is evidenced by the corporate wellness programs that have become part of the employee benefits offering of many companies worldwide. What's different now is that the intensity of the mental stress and suffering so many people endured through the pandemic (and are still experiencing), threw a spotlight on the issue, and has catalysed the need for more serious attention.

Historically speaking, it's not unusual in organizations of any size (from startup to large, publicly traded companies) that some employees will experience and suffer from a measure of stress and/or anxiety even under regular circumstances. Of course I'm not advocating that this should be considered a norm—it shouldn't—but the reality is that many, if not most people, live with some level of stress, whether it be work-related, personal or both.

Now throw a global pandemic into the mix, with people being required to work, learn, and live at home—facing massive and constant uncertainty under often tremendously challenging circumstances—and the stress bubble comes close to bursting. Top this off with job-related challenges such as problematic relationships with co-workers, funding issues, salary sacrifices, furloughs or pending retrenchments... the list is infinite, and the stress is constantly compounding.

Even in the distant past of February 2020—what used to be considered "normal" times—it was understood that when people suffer from anxiety, they are likely to be somewhat to significantly less effective and productive than their more laidback colleagues.

But while awareness of mental health matters and their impact on the workplace started receiving more attention in recent years, until COVID struck, the reigning mentality continued to be one of "Keep Calm and Carry On." However, many lessons were learned about mental illness in the pandemic—lessons that will continue to leave their mark into the future, and will hopefully ensure greater awareness of, and response to, struggling employees.

Probably the most salient insight that can be taken from this time is that we all have a basic need for routine and certainty in order for our nervous systems to be able to function optimally. Constantly being in a state of high alert, and expecting danger and upheaval as a matter of course, do not make the best foundation for workplace excellence. It is therefore incumbent on leaders to provide as much safety and certainty to their teams as possible.

Here's how:

FLEXIBLE ROUTINE

Regardless of where you land on your decision-making about your company or team's remote or in-office setup, ensure this is linked to a set routine, whatever that may be. Even if you allow your colleagues to choose what works best for them, this trust in your staff should not equate to a "Free for All". Total autonomy would be counterproductive in any event, because it would be destabilizing for everyone. Flexibility does not require the complete annihilation of boundaries and structure.

COMMUNICATION

Continue to communicate regularly regarding milestones and expectations, so that people can plan their lives and achieve a greater degree of certainty. For example, if you intend to be an all-in-the-office team from the time that everyone is vaccinated, make that clear. If you plan to have a four-day work week, or a hot-desk setup—or anything else at all—communicate this as soon as you can.

Even if you're not yet sure about the path you'll be taking, share this too. In my experience, little to no communication creates anxiety - whereas frequent engagement, even if it's to share that you still don't know, puts people at greater ease.

REASSURANCE

People are usually very fearful about losing their jobs. For those who have made it this far, they may still be living with the constant fear that this day could be their last—particularly if your company has already undergone retrenchments. Although it may be impossible to offer any real certainty around the future, letting your people know they can be assured of their jobs under x, y and z conditions, can go a long way to having them breathe more easily. It also shifts their focus from their anxiety about the future, to the deadlines of today.

Now let's talk about how to handle mental health issues.

Are you feeling stressed, anxious, burnt out, exhausted, feeling a bit depressed or under the weather? If you're currently in a leadership role, I'm willing to bet that you've said yes to at least two or three on this list. And, without any hesitation of doubt, some of your staff are likely suffering from some of these mental health issues too.

Yes, I said it. Mental Health. Here's the thing: many of us have been functioning with varying degrees of these maladies, assuming they're an intrinsic element of work, as opposed to an issue of mental health. The language of mental wellness and mental illness (the state that arises when we become dysfunctional due to the above-mentioned issues) has been somewhat 'off limits' until recently. People are far more willing to acknowledge being ill and put themselves 'off work' due to a physical ailment than due to an overload of stress and anxiety. So you can bet that there's a lot more mental-emotional unwellness happening in your organisation than you know about.

And yet, increasingly leaders are having the conversation about mental well-being in their workplaces now, primarily 'thanks' to the pandemic.

The sustainability of pandemic-style productivity gains might well depend on how organizational leaders address the anxiety their employees feel—and the associated levels of burnout[4].

---

4 "What Executives Are Saying about the Future of Hybrid Work." McKinsey & Company. McKinsey & Company, June 8, 2021. https://www.mckinsey.com/business-functions/organization/our-insights/what-executives-are-saying-about-the-future-of-hybrid-work?cid=other-eml-nsl-mip-mck&hlkid=22f64a2f129542a5950a0dc7f58c2385&hctky=11601495&hdpid=ceff44f0-dfbd-435e-ac8c-852e9afcf44f.

What's evident as time passes, is that the ongoing pressure and daily challenges in some individuals' lives due to the pandemic (be it ill family members, children who are not yet in a proper school routine due to COVID-related school closures, anxiety about new virus variants and how to protect against these, or adjusting to back-to-office plans that may no longer suit new lifestyles) has taken its toll, even for those who seemed to have been coping with relative ease during the height of the pandemic.

People have become exhausted. Some are at breaking point. All the extra energy required to plan, work around, adapt, change—and then repeat (multiple times) when what had been planned for must change YET AGAIN—is just... exhausting! Mental fatigue alone has worn people down, resulting in burnout, lack of motivation, and general malaise.

And, as much as leaders themselves have been affected by all of the above (you're not spared any of the above just because you're an executive), it's nevertheless up to leaders to pay proper attention to the issues that impact their teams and their organisations, and then to act.

Some of the everyday steps leaders can implement to support staff to maintain emotional and mental wellness include:

- **Regular personal care calls/check-ins.** In the early days of COVID, everyone was very focused on communication. Lots of it... with at least some focused on personal wellbeing. By communicating (and sometimes over-communicating), leaders were able to get a pulse check on their teams, and address fears, concerns and anxieties as soon as they arose.

With time, the focus shifted to business as usual via video, and the calls to check on people and how they were doing were replaced by standard meetings (internal and external), with less attention placed on individual wellbeing. Some people managed to adjust satisfactorily to new ways of remote working, but those who didn't, suffered—often in silence. So whether staff are in the office, or still working remotely, start making personal care calls or face-to-face check-ins a feature of the new work normal going forward.

- **Regular wellness breaks and more leave.** Very few can claim to have taken the kind of proper breaks or vacations needed to rest and rejuvenate. People may have taken a few days off work here and there, but the intended impact of coming back to work with the energy and drive to push hard again is just not there for most.

  Additionally, the imperative to make up for time lost as business starts to resuscitate has seen people being pushed—or pushing themselves—to unhealthy hours at work. Let's get real: of course it's tempting to make up for lost time and revenue, but people are not robots, and as the saying goes, 'All work and no play makes Jack a dull boy.' So don't do it! And the only real antidote to the pervasive sense of fatigue that is likely to have crept in (if it even left in the first place), is to ensure staff have adequate access to time off.

Some smart companies have already instituted enforced breaks, like designating the last Friday of every month as a leave day for the whole company. Others are offering unlimited leave (with conditions), rotating leave for teams, or half days. So figure out a leave strategy that might work for your organization, and try it out for a period. You need not make it a company policy forever—just beta test it, and see how people respond.

- **Counselling and wellness support.** For those companies that have the budget and infrastructure, it would be a great step in the right direction to invest in psychological counselling (at the company's expense) for those who need it. Another option might be group support sessions facilitated by trained coaches.

The primary challenge here is dealing with the 'denial' hurdle. I've seen many companies (including my own) offer everything from individual psychotherapy to life coaching, and yet the uptake is slow. People remain reluctant to admit that they're struggling emotionally, and those who need the support the most often shy away from taking the help on offer.

The manner in which this benefit is provided is critical—the promise of confidentiality and non-judgement must be ironclad, and a solid bedrock of trust in relationships between management and staff is essential.

Notwithstanding the challenges, implementing some of the strategies outlined above will cost relatively little, and will likely offer a significant increase in health and wellbeing of your teams.

And for those who may need business fundamentals to support the human fundamentals, there is an abundance of data showing how the mental and emotional wellbeing of your people will have a significant impact on your company's performance and growth—hence the integration of compassion and commerciality makes perfect sense.

CHAPTER 7

MANAGING INEQUALITY IN THE HYBRID

IN RELATION TO THE GLOBAL PANDEMIC, THE STATEMENT "WE'RE all in the same boat" was recognized as false by almost everyone in any work environment that included mothers of young children, and anyone not comfortably ensconced in the middle-to-upper working class. Undoubtedly, these groups faced huge challenges not encountered by those who were more well-off, or were able to operate from a laptop in their living room without rushing to aid homeschoolers every 10 minutes.

THE LOST YEAR FOR WOMEN WITH CAREERS

The data now shows unquestionably that women with young children have been the ones to feel the greatest strain during COVID. In 2020, a significant percentage of women needed to opt out of the workplace or reduce their hours to take on the bulk of childcare and home-schooling during the worst stages of lockdown. For those women who soldiered on, career growth was, in some cases, stunted. This was due to them having to decline promotions, or them not being considered eligible for promotions they were due (had the additional stresses of work-from-home not become so painfully evident to the powers that be).

According to US data aggregated by financial media platform Robinhood Snacks:

- More than two and a half million women dropped out of the labor force between February 2020 and January 2021, compared to just under two million men.
- Women's labor force participation rate stands at 56%—its lowest level since 1987—with women of color particularly affected.
- As of January 2021, there were 4.8% fewer Black women in the labor force than a year ago—compared with a 3.1% drop for white women.

On the whole, the pandemic of 2020 was a dagger in the heart for women in leadership, the quantum of which will become clear well into the future. Needless to say, if serious attention is not paid to this challenge, the gains in gender diversity and parity that have been made in workplaces globally, may suffer irrevocably.

The question that every leader should be seriously asking themselves, their executive teams, and their diversity officers, is how to stem the tide, and stop the freefall. As it stands, there is a strong case to be made for addressing the lost year that was 2020 for women with careers.

PAY ATTENTION. BE FAIR.

It goes without saying (but just in case, I'm saying it again) that leaders need to continue to pay close attention to the context in which their employees live and operate. Understand the logistics of their everyday lives as it impacts on their ability to perform. These factors will be at play far into, what is likely to be, a hybrid-work model future.

COVID has magnified inequalities between those who have the home environment, infrastructure, bandwidth, devices and support that have allowed them to continue on a positive career trajectory, and those without—who continue to battle, simply to stay afloat.

The notion of being able to leave one's personal life at the door when arriving at work is no longer possible (not that it was ever a particularly sound foundation for a healthy company culture). Instead of being expected to leave one's personal life at home, personal circumstances need to be fully taken into account in a much more deliberate, intentional and holistic way.

KEEP INEQUALITY AWAY FROM THE HYBRID

As we head back into some kind of hybrid work setup, we will need to be particularly aware of those in our organisations who still want and need (for health reasons) to remain very careful in terms of COVID vulnerabilities. This includes those employees caring for vulnerable family members, or children who have not yet returned to school.

These individuals may not want, or be able to, join meetings at the office, travel, and so forth. Logistics around meetings, team building sessions, and retreats must be considered fairly where some members of the team may not be ready to connect yet. What judgments (overt or tacit) are passed on the work-from-homers? How might it impact their involvement in decision-making when they are not physically present?

On the opposite end of the scale, some companies may have decided to sustain working from home as a company policy into the future—whether for cost saving purposes, or because this suits the majority of employees who may have enjoyed the flexibility offered by the new way of working. What needs to be taken into consideration in these situations is the plight of the minority who may prefer to go to an office to do their work—either because their home set up is not conducive to optimal productivity, or because they thrive amidst the social interaction and collaboration of working in the same building as their peers.

Indeed, the desire, willingness or ability to be in the office with colleagues is a key factor that is likely to disrupt the equilibrium as we return to some measure of routine in the coming months.

Concerns on the part of employees (those who want to work in person, and those who can't or don't want to) should not be written off, and unequivocal policies will not suffice in the quest for creating a fair and equal workplace. As ethical leaders, committed to growing workplace diversity at all levels, we are required to consider the individual circumstances of members of our teams, and accommodate and compensate for them to the best of our ability.

Gender, race and other inequalities will continue to play a role going forward, and leaders must be proactive to ensure personal circumstances impacting employees are recognised and accounted for. Individual circumstances quite often have more of an impact on performance and productivity than innate capability and commitment—particularly when said performance is taking place at home as opposed to in the office.

Most companies have taken company or team-wide surveys to assess willingness and preferences around the work environment, and they are already starting to manage expectations around the future. However, there is an additional level of attention that needs to be applied by leaders to unanticipated and unintended inequalities that could creep in to even the most well-intentioned plans.

Here are some of the key points to note and consider:

- What negative judgments are being made about otherwise productive and valuable team members who are expressing the need to continue to work from home, and what might the consequences be for promotions, project allocations, and bonuses?
- What consideration is being given to those who want to go to an office to work in instances where physical office space has been indefinitely terminated?

- What additional support still needs to be provided in order to fully democratize whatever new hybrid solution is being considered for the future?
- What inequalities (overt or subtle) have infiltrated your team or organization during COVID that now need attention in order for redress to happen?

This challenge is complex, and even when one knows the questions to ask, the answers are seldom clear-cut. While it may seem easier to govern groups with clear rules, the future is going to require many exceptions to the rule, and an approach of leading with equitable principles and frameworks. My hope is that leaders will be willing to experiment with new ideas, even if it means that there may be some missteps along the way.

"What good is an idea if it remains an idea?

Try. Experiment. Iterate. Fail. Try again. Change the world."

—Simon Sinek

CHAPTER 8

DRIVING DIVERSITY THROUGH YOUR HIRING STRATEGY

MANY WILL LOOK BACK ON 2020 AS THE YEAR IN WHICH diversity in the workplace received not just a nod, but a "hell yes!" from corporate America. On the agenda for some time, but never realized, the move toward diversity was well and truly fast-tracked by the rise of the Black Lives Matter movement—the reverberations of which were experienced globally. COVID and driving diversity will somehow remain inextricably interlinked. 2020 will be remembered as a defining moment in history in which diversity—particularly at leadership levels—became a non-negotiable in some of the most powerful organizations in the world.

"Only when diverse perspectives are included, respected and valued can we start to get a full picture of the world."

—BRENE BROWN

With additional historic exclamation points, such as the election of Kamala Harris as US Vice President, we find ourselves in a position where we can proceed with renewed hope for diversity and inclusion, both in politics and in the corporate world. Yet, as we all know, hope is not going to do the trick when it comes to sustainable shifts and changes in organizations. Especially those who have clung onto the status quo despite the tidal wave of evidence—and moral imperative—in support of diversity.

Nigerian gay rights activist Bisi Alimi distils the challenge of entrenched organizational inequality quite simply in saying, "What has been coming back over and over and over again is that at the entry level you have more women and minorities. By the time they get to the middle-management level, the white men are overtaking them. And by the time they get to the senior management level, the women are missing, the Blacks are missing. This structure is set up like running a race with obstacles on the way, while your opponent is running the same race on the smooth ground. And you have to finish at the same time."

This view is reflected in almost every diversity study out there, including one conducted by our research team at Jack Hammer in conjunction with contributors from Harvard Business School in 2019. The study looked at the CEO makeup of Fortune 1000 companies, focusing on the women in these roles, in order to determine common trends, patterns, traits or characteristics that could reveal a pathway to success for aspirant female CEOs.

What jumps out like a lightning bolt is the first data point of the study—namely the percentage of female CEOs in these companies.

Six.

As in six percent...

Admittedly, this is just one data set and one sample pool, and focuses only on the question of gender diversity. But it happens to be the sample pool containing some of the largest organizations in the world. If you were to look at other groupings of companies, the ratios might be somewhat less alarming. But not entirely so. Regardless of which group of large publicly traded companies you analyse in the world (bar a couple of outliers), I guarantee you'll find a pretty big difference in the number of male-led vs female-led ones.

And so here we are, at a moment in time when we have hope, a significant groundswell in activist voices, and an abundance of data driving diversity. This coincides with a work world that has gone through one of the most defining periods of global transition in modern history—paving the way for some real change.

Whether change can and will be effected is going to depend as heavily on the systemic issues—that are the 'obstacles on the way' as referenced by Alimi—as it will on the strategic and executional parts of hiring, development and retention of diverse leaders in organizations.

And the hiring strategy and process is a foundational function where every single leader has an opportunity to impact change.

Most organizations have changed their hiring processes, but leading companies have reimagined them entirely[5].

---

5 "What Executives Are Saying about the Future of Hybrid Work." McKinsey & Company. McKinsey & Company, June 8, 2021. https://www.mckinsey.com/business-functions/ organization/our-insights/what-executives-are-saying-about-the-future-of-hybrid-work?cid=other-eml-nsl-mip-mck&hlkid=22f64a2f129542a5950a0dc7f58c2385&hctk y=11601495&hdpid=ceff44f0-dfbd-435e-ac8c-852e9afcf44f.

ARTICULATE DELIBERATE INTENTION AND COMMITMENT TO DIVERSE HIRING THROUGHOUT THE COMPANY

The one small—but critical—step needed from the outset that will dramatically impact diversity hiring for every single organization that follows it, is the articulation of intent. I've witnessed how frequently this articulation and communication of intention is missed. The CEO may know it. The HR director and talent sourcing team may know it. But unless everyone—and in particular every hiring manager—is aware of the commitment to ensuring a diversified pool of candidates to interview AND hire, it is highly likely that the extra steps needed to expand the talent pool accordingly will not be taken.

The result is the default hiring of the best candidates who applied for the job, in terms of historical metrics that do nothing to advance the intention to expand the diversity at leadership levels. There is nothing wrong with hiring the best person for the job, of course. Except that if none of the "best people" for the job were diversity candidates, the opportunity to shift the needle by recruiting diverse teams is then lost.

CHANGE YOUR SOURCING STRATEGY FOR DIFFERENT OUTCOMES

It's not rocket science to state that making concrete changes in the demographic makeup of your company is going to require changes to the talent pool you're sourcing from. To change the composition of your talent pool, you're probably going to need to change your sourcing strategy.

Try a quick candidate search on one of the large job boards in order to see what I mean. Almost any search for senior managers and executives will show a pool of talent that is significantly skewed—with women being under-represented (20% or less) in every technical or commercial role category. Add some ethnic diversity to this and the numbers are even more dismal!

So if companies rely on a recruitment strategy that focuses purely on sourcing active applicants (candidates who respond to a job post, or those who have made it clear they're on the market), utilising the large job boards, they're going to continue to miss out on the opportunity to interview high-quality diversity candidates.

Further, if a reliance on networking has been a sound strategy in the past, that is probably not going to be effective here either (unless the executive team or board has a well-developed network within the target demographic groups).

A MULTI-PRONGED APPROACH TO HIRING FOR DIVERSITY

- It starts at the top—diversify the board
    There is ample research to show that when the non-executive board is diversified, there is a much greater likelihood of a diverse CEO hire, and consequently a diverse executive team hiring.

In the past, board appointments were mostly made through the "buddy system." Meaning, somebody knows someone who knows someone within the group's known network. If there's one sure way of sustaining the status quo, it's this!

More and more frequently these days, board appointments are taking place by using executive search firms to access a broader pool of talent. This can be a sound strategy and one that works well if the executive search firm itself is known for diversity appointments, and has a track record of helping companies build leadership teams and boards that have a wider range of genders, ethnicities, sexualities and backgrounds.

"Companies with a high representation of women board members significantly outperformed those with no female directors."

–CATALYST ANALYSIS

Which brings me to my next point…

- Ensure that the executive search firm driving the hiring process is diverse

  There is a greater likelihood of attracting a varied talent pool to the table when the people entrusted with the hiring process are diverse themselves. Want more top women, people of color, or LGBTQ+ leaders on your shortlist? Want access to leaders who will buy into the narrative around change and progress? You may want to consider being thoughtful about who your search partners are, and how they're representing your organization to the pool of talent that you want to engage with.

Which brings me to my next point…

- You're going to need to proactively reach out to the talent you want—work with professionals who know how to do this!

  The ONLY way to really change the game is to proactively identify and reach out to potential candidates. If you prefer not to work with an executive search firm to do this for you (affordability can certainly be an issue), then make sure you're allocating adequate resources (time and people) to do this work. Consider it a priority project that will require a considerable investment to have the desired impact.

Also…

- Consider talent pipelining to effect long term change

    Talent pipelining is a style of recruiting that is often utilized for lower level, multi-hire positions in an organization, but the principles of this proactive recruitment strategy can be applied equally well to board or senior leadership level roles.

    A talent pipelining initiative will enable you to have a pool of potential (diverse) prospects waiting in the wings when you're ready to appoint. By identifying high-quality candidates, and then engaging with them around future potential roles, you have the opportunity to build relationships with candidates over time, conduct referencing, and assess fit for rapid appointment when the time is right.

    A project of this nature can be done using your internal resources, but is best with an external partner who has this as their focus. I've seen companies become very enthusiastic about this initiative and allocate resources to it for a short while, but only until other "more urgent" matters take over and the talent pipelining work falls entirely off the radar.

So, to my final point…

- It's a marathon, not a sprint

    None of these hiring strategies can take place over-night—or indeed, make a difference to your company's diversity in the short-term. All are medium to long term strategies for diverse leadership. But to get there from here, the point is that you need to **start now**—by getting your strategy ironed out, and then by taking one or more of the above steps. You will certainly start seeing a difference in the future.

CHAPTER 9

EVP: THE CRITICAL DIFFERENTIATOR TO ATTRACT FUTURE TALENT

YOUR EVP (EMPLOYEE VALUE PROPOSITION) HAS NEVER BEEN more important to define and effectively communicate than it is now. As we emerge from the worst stages of the pandemic into some form of hybrid work-life, and as economies rebound, the demand for talent is intensifying daily. In my conversations with leaders all over the world (in large corporations and VC-backed startups alike), they all state hiring talent as one of their top three challenges.

Add to this surge in the demand for skills, the imperative to diversify the talent pool and the competition for the best available talent is on the boil. In the past year, hiring slowed down apart from the most critical appointments. But with light now appearing at the end of the tunnel, talent attraction is once more top of mind, and gears must shift quickly.

The way high-quality candidates make decisions about their future has changed, and emerging as one of the key differentiators in the talent attraction process, is the value, purpose and meaning that your company offers to its employees.

Yes, read that again. To attract the best people out there, you'll need to demonstrate how YOUR COMPANY adds value to the lives of its employees beyond just salary and benefits.

And, what may have sufficed as a solid EVP pre-COVID may no longer cut the mustard. Indeed this, like most other aspects of our working world, has changed and needs to be re-evaluated.

"Beyond doing the right thing for their workers, companies have another reason to lean into workforce development initiatives: their own competitiveness.
As demand for skills for the intelligent era heat up, so too will a war for talent."

—SARAH FRANKLIN
Salesforce CMO

For instance, before the pandemic, one of the EVPs often cited by more progressive companies in a bid to attract talent, was some kind of work-from-home concession or arrangement. Today, that is no longer an EVP, but rather an expected working arrangement in some form or another.

Further, my interviews with leaders reveal that this last year has been an intensely introspective time for many, resulting in a re-evaluation of priorities and greater clarity about how they want to spend the next phase of their work life.

What kind of work? What impact in the world? What type of work culture and team? These are the questions that people have been asking themselves, and many have come to the conclusion that a good salary at the end of the month is no longer enough of a consideration. More and more people are seeking to gain meaning (rather than just money) from their daily work. And we're not just talking about millennials and Generation Z here. It's across the board, with great performers now more likely than ever to seriously consider joining one company over another because of the potential to make a meaningful contribution.

People who wouldn't previously have been willing to take a call from a headhunter, for instance, all of a sudden clear their diaries for an interview when a company's brand or EVP is meaningful to them.

And here's the really important nuance. "Meaningful" and "impressive" have shifted from being great behemoths who are named on the Fortune 500 or 1000, to companies that stand for a cause or impact that resonates with candidates.

Undoubtedly, the most attractive companies these days are those who have social impact hardwired in their DNA—in their mission and vision—in a truly authentic way.

Here's the kicker—people are not naive. They can smell the lack of authenticity with companies who claim to have a mission to save the world in some way, but whose *de facto* business dealings and operations are inconsistent with their mission.

And similarly, when a company's vision is coherent and consistent with their actual work in the world, it's exceptionally powerful from a talent attraction and retention perspective.

These kinds of companies are like gold. They are able harness the power of their mission (not just their brand) to be talent magnets, and are able to attract the best of the best **because they have managed to communicate this effectively.**

BRING YOUR COMPANY'S BEST TO THE HIRING TABLE

But what if your company manufactures pillows, or services computer screens, or digitizes workflows? There are a gazillion companies out there whose lines of business are not, on the face of it, mission-driven. Do you give up and go for the bargain basement offering on the employee front? Or even outsource to distant shores, where the price tag is more attractive, given the ability to do so now that much work is remote?

The short answer is no. There's still tremendous opportunity to be impactful and contribute in a positive way to society regardless of your field, and also ensure that you hire the right people for YOUR company, not just the ones who can tick the productivity boxes.

In the world out there, I see companies addressing the above challenges in the following ways:

- They align their brand with a cause that is congruent with their core business, and ensure that there is meaningful and cohesive partnering.
- They contribute to charities or philanthropic initiatives—financially, as well as offering staff resources and investment. And they weave this charitable engagement into the fabric of as many customer touchpoints as possible.

GET TO GRIPS WITH THE CHANGED LANDSCAPE

It's important to understand that now that fancy offices with staff buffets, flexibility to work from home and related benefits are *de rigueur* (or of absolutely no interest whatsoever), the usual selling points no longer have the WOW factor they held before.

A year ago, candidates may have stated that they want to reduce their commute and travel time, with flexible work options to such a degree that they would consider a career move to make it happen. That is no longer a stand out opportunity, indeed, that is the starting point. So companies must now dig deep (with outside help if needed), to determine what actual value they offer to prospective candidates.

On the bright side for purpose-driven startups, this has levelled the playing field, as they are now in a better position to attract top talent who would have weighed up these (now basic) company benefits against the larger players.

Some of the new considerations that could entice a heavy hitter to your company include:

- The prospect that a candidate might feel they are making a meaningful contribution by way of their daily work
- Employee opportunities to participate in Corporate Social Investment initiatives or philanthropic investment
- Diversity initiatives
- Quality mentorship programs
- The prospect of personal and professional development
- Innovative leave policies
- A strong company focus on mental and emotional wellbeing
- An 'employee wallet', offering a monthly or annual sum that is available for employees to use as they wish, in the context of wellness-related benefits. This is a great way to hyper-personalize wellness benefits, and will have a very good likelihood of uptake by employees who are being given autonomy and choice in their own wellbeing.

Regardless of the size of your organisation, know that VALUE and MEANING matter to an increasing number of candidates out there. That's not to say that you won't find people who are happy to take an offer of a secure job at a nice company, where the boss doesn't shout at them and they get three weeks paid leave.

But in the race for TOP talent, purpose and mission-driven companies, with well-defined benefits that are geared to adding value to employees' lives are the ones that are winning! And if you can infuse into this a leadership model of love and loyalty, you'll be on the podium collecting gold for 'best company to work for'.

So if you have been struggling to find, place and retain the best talent, an objective consideration of the external perceptions about your company may be a worthwhile place to start.

And an even more worthwhile investment of time is to establish a well-defined, authentic brand and company promise to your current and future employees, in the context of a new world of work.

CHAPTER 10

REMOTE INTERVIEWING: GETTING TO KNOW THE REAL PERSON BEHIND THE SCREEN

IF YOU RECALL ALL THE WAY BACK IN CHAPTER 3, I ALLUDED to the fact that well-functioning, productive and engaged teams rely heavily on having the right people in the right roles. In other words, hiring for fit is the critical variable in the whole equation. Leaders who hire the right people (the ones who are the best fit for the role) are undoubtedly the winners when it comes to being able to cultivate the types of culture that supports their vision of success.

Whether success means high growth, fanatical customer loyalty, or a culture of love and loyalty (or any other, for that matter), hiring the right people who are well-suited and aligned with these goals and drivers is key.

I'm not going to dig into too much detail on hiring principles in this book, but it would be remiss of me not to share some of the game-changers and trends in hiring that have arisen due to the pandemic, and which are likely to sustain into the hybrid future.

Firstly, let's assume that remote interviewing is here to stay. Now that we've all been conducting interviews in this manner for the last year or so, and making appointments without ever having met candidates face-to-face, it's clear that it's not just doable, but in many ways, preferable to pre-COVID, in-person interviews.

Efficiency, time and cost savings are without question hugely tangible benefits. The ability to have high-level executive candidates meet with high-level board members without anyone needing to get on a plane, is undoubtedly one of COVID's greatest benefits.

Remote interviewing as the norm is a great development if—and this is a big if—interviewing skills are honed and on point, and all of the basics are covered and then adapted for digital engagement.

WHY IS INTERVIEWING SO CHALLENGING IN THE FIRST PLACE?

We all know that there is a tremendous amount of artifice and game-playing that takes place in an interview. Everyone is on their best behaviour, and everyone aims to present themselves in the best possible light. It's a courting ritual, a masquerade ball, a show. And as a result, it's a tough task which requires time and skill, but crucially, experience and the ability to identify what lies beneath, what sits behind the best-interview-behaviour mask. There are many layers to get through, to determine what is real and what is not.

That is one of the core objectives of an interview—to get beyond the surface of that which is offered in the candidate's CV, to determine not just whether the candidate is qualified and suitably experienced, but also whether they are RIGHT for the role, the company, and the team in which they'll operate, or lead.

HOW VIDEO CHANGED SOME PARTS OF THE GAME

These days, with interviewing people in their homes, we've managed to take a little peek behind the curtain, so to speak. The masquerade is somewhat tempered due to seeing people in their own (likely more casual) familiar surroundings. One layer of the onion has already been peeled away, enabling everyone—both interviewer and candidate—to connect and experience each other in a less artificial way, outside of the neutral sterility of the office environment.

On the one hand, this can be considered (another) one of the unanticipated benefits of COVID hiring. On the other hand, an even greater alert needs to be sounded on the increased levels of unconscious bias that might be at play when one is interviewing people in their homes.

In the past, meeting people in the office provided a relatively neutral and equal setting for the interview. Hopefully, most interviewers had already embarked on a process of becoming attuned to the unconscious bias at play with appearance and attire of candidates, diction and intonation, and other non-job-related personal attributes. Hopefully, they had also become aware of additional possible biases based on common networks and affiliations, educational background and so on.

AWARENESS OF BIAS

What was entirely new for many who had not previously interviewed candidates in their home setting, was the impact of a candidate's surroundings on bias.

Everything from being able to take a peek at the book titles on the bookshelf, to the religious, spiritual or motivational posters on the wall, to the certificates of achievement or photos of babies in the side view, was now at play in the judgment game. Whether unconsciously or consciously, the home setting for interviews provided enormous potential for the interview to become an even greater judgment, and bias-inducing fest.

Firstly, in order to make really great hiring decisions and hire the right fit for your company, you're going to need to develop an awareness of bias—shifting your unconscious into the realms of awareness. This helps ensure your decision-making is rooted in **structured and behavioural-based** interviewing, as opposed to intuition or gut feelings based on external markers that were not present in the pre-COVID era.

What happens too frequently is that fit is loosely interpreted as, "Do I like this person?" Or, "Is this candidate on a similar energetic vibe or wavelength as me?" and, "Is there good chemistry or rapport?" We know that when a candidate and an interviewer have mutual interests, know the same people, or have other points of connection (such as school, college, town, country, religion), there is an increased likelihood of a sense of rapport being created. And it's when rapport or chemistry is mistaken for fit that hiring problems arise.

GET CLEAR ON VALUES-BASED INTERVIEWING

Secondly, in the quest of hiring for fit when you're exclusively (or even partially) interviewing candidates remotely, you're going to need to get clear on your organisation's core values.

Without a detailed analysis and definition of the values of the company (which can be loosely defined as a set of beliefs and behaviours of the people who work in the company), interviewing for fit, whether in person or via Zoom, will always be hit and miss.

Furthermore, not only is it key to DEFINE the values of the company, but also to understand what they mean IN PRACTICE.

Now let's take this into the interview process.

Assume that the company has gone through a thorough process to define the company values, and to gain clarity on their interpretation and meaning in the context of the organization. In other words, everyone is clear about what the words on the posters on the walls mean in terms of expected (and lived) behaviours in the company.

When interviewing for fit, the job of the interviewer is to assess whether the candidate displays the mindset and behaviours that align with those of the organization.

How do you do this?

Develop a few questions that will demonstrate how the candidate behaves in certain circumstances. This will then determine whether there's a value match, and hence, whether there's a good fit.

HERE IS AN EXAMPLE:

Jack Hammer's core values are:

- Perform to win
- Look beyond the obvious
- Build connection

Each of these has an explanation and description of what they mean.

Perform to win is most certainly NOT to win at all costs. Instead, this value is about striving for excellence, and pushing hard to succeed for our clients and our candidates. It's less about being competitive internally, and much more about winning for our key stakeholders.

To assess if a candidate has a similar mindset, we ask questions like:

- Tell about a situation where you put your client's needs ahead of your own.
- Give an example of going the extra mile on a project.
- Share a story about how you've worked competitively in a team.

Note that all of these require the candidate to share an example or a story. This then gives you the opportunity to drill into this by asking open-ended questions such as "tell me more," "help me understand," or "unpack this for me..."

Do this for all of your core values, and you'll have a VERY clear idea about whether the candidate will be a good fit for your team or company.

Does that sound like hard work? Well, it is. It takes time, preparation, thought, and diligence to frame all the questions, and thereafter to probe deeply when you hear answers that are different to what you expected. There are few black-and-white answers here, and so this part of the interview process is a real investment of time and energy.

LEVERAGE COVID-STYLE LEADERSHIP TO ASSESS SKILLS AND FIT

Another unintended silver lining for hiring managers, is how this time in history can (and will most certainly in the future) be used to evaluate leadership skills and attributes.

If you're of the view that the way in which a leader showed up in the past—particularly under highly stressful circumstances—is a pretty good indicator of how they will behave or function in future similar situations, then digging deep into a leader's COVID track record will be invaluable in evaluating a number of leadership traits.

In no particular order these would include: agility and versatility, fluidity and flexibility, innovation and creativity, empathy and EQ, decision-making and judgment, communication and stakeholder engagement, and delegation. Not to mention temperament—particularly in the ability of a leader to sympathetically but also effectively support and manage productivity and performance under the most difficult of circumstances.

Many leaders who had taken on senior roles after the Global Financial Crisis of 2008 have not really had to prove their mettle under extreme circumstances.

Until 2020 of course, more than a decade later. And how illuminating this time has been! For those of us who have been around long enough to have worked our way through a global crisis or two, what we know well is how extreme circumstances like these offer the opportunity to gain very real insights into the makeup and constitution of a leader. Asking pointed questions and extracting examples about how the leader handled herself, her team, and her key stakeholders during this challenging time will be exceptionally revealing, and a key to determining future leadership appointments.

REMOTE INTERVIEWING NUGGETS

I interviewed many leaders who told me stories about how they made some really great quality hires during the last year. They attribute this to three main factors:

- Increased awareness of unconscious bias, particularly due to the increase in diversity training that was taking place during 2020 – 2021.

- More time to interview in the early days of COVID— before the workday became a back-to-back Zoom nightmare, many people found themselves with more time in their schedules, and a little more time to allocate to their candidate interviews.

- Greater focus on conducting structured interviews, due to the digital channel. The change of environment meant that interviewers needed to pay more attention to the way in which they were interviewing. Old patterns, interview styles and habits were given a shakeup and, on the whole, interviewers felt that their interview skills had sharpened during COVID.

For those hoping to find the key for interviewing and hiring the right fit, here it is—become aware of your bias, allocate sufficient time (meaning, more than you used to take—this is not an activity to be rushed or squeezed into short gaps) and conduct structured interviews, particularly when it comes to fit.

There's little difference between in-person and remote interviewing, because if you're truly relying on a structured interview process as opposed to the chemistry that you thought was such a help back in the day, you're likely to always make considerably better, higher quality decisions. Allocate the right amount of time to the interview process and strip out unconscious bias, and you'll have found the holy grail of hiring for REAL fit, and substantially increase the odds of making great hiring decisions.

CONCLUSION

GIVEN THAT THE OFFICE NO LONGER DEFINES THE PLACE in which we work, and a hybrid future is here for at least the foreseeable future, leaders are going to need to apply themselves in new ways by taking the lessons already learned and readying themselves for those that are up ahead. Indeed, almost all of the structures and truths that we held about how, when and where work needed to take place, have imploded or been shown to have much greater range than we'd ever contemplated. Time zones and geographies are less important than they used to be with people having been empowered to make choices about where they work and during which hours of the day. Some choose to work from four in the morning, others choose the night hours.

And digital nomads are a real thing—and not just for millenial techies working in internet businesses. In many ways, we all had a taste of becoming an internet worker, in some cases being able to leverage the freedoms and possibilities that life not constrained by offices and schools provided.

So where are we now, and what are the trends pointing towards?

People want a personalized workplace experience that supports them as individuals. Having had a taste of this over the last year, there are expectations of ongoing flexibility and consideration for personal circumstances into the future. Without too much generalizing and categorizing, the feedback coming in loud and clear from surveys all over the world are showing, for example, that working parents (particularly the primary caregivers), are likely to want loads more flexibility and much less in-office time. The exception to this is parents who have domestic support, or those whose work-from-home situations are not conducive to productivity.

Some people (generally younger or single people) on the other hand, are much more keen for in-office time, except where this requires a long commute. They enjoy the social aspect of working in an office space, as well as some of the perks that might come along with some office environments.

There are also those who had a taste of digital nomad life, and would love to continue on this path. If they are able to arrive at virtual meetings prepared and at the required times, and deliver their work at the highest level on time, why not?

It's a real smorgasbord out there at this stage, and how far leaders are willing to go to accommodate preferences as a perk of the job, or even talent attraction and retention initiatives, remains to be seen.

The reality is that when it's no longer one-size-fits-all, it can make everyone's lives a lot more complex. Or not. There may be some very simple and elegant solutions to keeping everyone as happy (and productive) as possible in the new version of working in the hybrid.

Regardless of the way forward, whether it's work from home forever, four days in and one flexi, or all in (is anyone actually going to do that?)—the veil of the workplace has been lifted, the Wizard of Oz has been revealed, and we've all seen that it's possible, and in some cases preferable, to do things differently.

And now that we've all seen this, it's impossible to unsee. The result? It's expected that there will need to be a good rationale for future policies and procedures manuals, or the determination to stick with any kind of one-size-fits-all approach. Of course, they will continue to exist, some for good reason. So let's not get too hasty with throwing it all out. But without a doubt, there are great opportunities to drive innovation in relation to our people that would not previously have made it on the agenda.

Maternity leave policies, as an example, can be completely reshaped, and provide flexibility for everyone—enabling new moms the ability to take the time that they want with their newborns, while simultaneously choosing to commence work at month three or four (or even earlier, if it suits them). For that matter, why not allow new moms (or dads) to work from home for six months to a year after their baby arrives, provided they continue to deliver on their tasks?

Overall, companies and leaders have an opportunity to take a proper look at the employee experience in their organizations, and map career journeys in ways that would not have been thought possible pre-pandemic. For those who do—the ones who take the lessons into the hybrid future, and who take the time to really continue on a path of innovation—their companies will become talent magnets. Regardless of which work generation you fall into—Gen X, Y, Z or millennial (not forgetting the boomers)—everyone got a taste of alternatives.

And that's what they will want in the future. Options. So that they can make choices that are meaningful to them.

Undoubtedly, the companies and leaders who have internalized the lessons learnt in 2020 and continue to build towards a future-focused business, are best positioned to leverage their new competitive advantage to land and retain the best leaders and teams.

As mentioned earlier in the book, I have been under tremendous time pressure to finish *The Living Room Leader*. I can see that many leaders all over the world are very anxious to get back to normal, and while I too can't wait for a time when we can live without fear of falling ill, or infecting others, I am loath to go back and lose the positive gains that have been made in so many ways.

My intention with this book was (and is) to offer pause for thought to those who are passionate about becoming great leaders, and to provide an opportunity to reflect and consider what we have learnt during this tumultuous time—and then to take some of the lessons and apply them in our hybrid future.

If you've reached this final part of the book, I'm hopeful that you're part of the cohort of lifelong students of leadership, and that you've picked up at least one idea that you're excited to try out (or retain) with your team or company.

I also hope that by now you're in the fortunate position of being able to elect whether or not you'll continue to lead from your chosen room at home, or whether you'll perhaps be heading back to the office at some point, for some hours or days of the week.

Regardless of where you find yourself, my wish is that you lead well, with empathy, care and love, as we emerge into our hybrid future.

ACKNOWLEDGEMENTS

DURING THE MANY ANXIOUS MONTHS AFTER THE WORLD WENT into a global lockdown, I spent hours and hours on calls with leaders all over the world, trying to make sense of the impact of COVID-19 on every element of our emerging new work-life. As it turns out, there was not all that much sense to be had in what now feels like the early days of the ravaging pandemic—but I nevertheless owe deep gratitude to the many colleagues, clients, and work friends, who shared their inspiring stories with me.

Leading in a crisis is hard. Exceptionally so.

Showing up every day with a clear head (while dealing with one's own pandemic-induced challenges) to provide direction, guidance, support, solace, focus, motivation (and so much more), requires the most tremendous amount of fortitude, courage and creativity. Each and every one of the incredible humans I conversed with has this in bucket-loads. Most notably: Stephen van Coller, Gerrie Fourie, Katlego Maphai, Bongiwe Gangeni, Tayo Ovioso, Malisha Awunor, Jasmin Pillay, Buhle Goslar, Harley Kisberg, and Osai Ojhigo. Thank you for consistently demonstrating great leadership, regardless of which room in the house you happened to find yourselves.

And to Ella Smook, editor extraordinaire—for helping me to breathe life into *The Living Room Leader*, and for keeping me on track and focused throughout. It wouldn't have happened without you!

ABOUT THE AUTHOR

DEBBIE IS GROUP CEO OF JACK HAMMER, A GLOBAL GROUP of executive search, talent advisory and leadership coaching companies. These include: Jack Hammer USA (which focuses on disruptive and emerging industries), Jack Hammer Africa (Africa's largest executive search boutique), Virtual Coaching Partners (an online leadership coaching platform) and ontheBLOCK (talent consulting for blockchain companies).

For the last 20 years, she has been helping boards and CEOs—from large established companies and NPOs to VC-backed start-ups—with their most important people, leadership and talent decisions. After all these years, her highest excitement comes from working with some of the world's most progressive leaders, cultivating amazing workplaces where everyone thrives.

Debbie currently acts as Advisor to several blockchain and crypto VC funds, and to Rebel Girls (a global multi-platform girl-driven edutainment company); she also coaches founder-CEOs who want to accelerate their leadership skills as their companies scale and grow.

Her first book (on team culture), "IntheFlow – Taking Mindfulness to Work", was listed in the 'Top 10 Best' South African business books. Debbie is a serial entrepreneur, with a somewhat unconventional background: In her 'first' career, she was an award-winning contemporary dancer and choreographer... whilst completing her law degree.

"As much as I loved being a professional dancer, I have found tremendous creativity in the world of business and leadership. The rigor and mastery required is extraordinarily intense, but utterly rewarding. Just like being a dancer!"

CPSIA information can be obtained
at www.ICGtesting.com
Printed in the USA
LVHW030819091021
699964LV00001B/6